Improve your practice!

Piano

Paul Harris

www.fabermusic.com/improve

© 2004 by Faber Music Ltd
First published in 2004 by Faber Music Ltd
3 Queen Square London WC1N 3AU
Design by Susan Clarke
Printed in England by Caligraving Ltd

ISBN 0-571-52261-0

FABER _ff_ MUSIC

Introduction

You've probably heard the expression 'practice makes perfect'. But it's not just the quantity of practice that's important; it's the quality. With the aid of *Improve your practice!*, you will begin to develop ways of making the most out of your practice sessions – however long they are. What's more, you'll also find that your wider musical skills of aural, theory, sight-reading, improvisation and composition develop alongside. And the fun playing cards are guaranteed to liven things up no end! So good luck, and let's get started ...

Here's what you do:

Before you start
Get out your scissors and cut each playing card to size. As you work through each grade, add the new cards to your deck so you have even more to choose from.

1 Be a musical detective
When you begin a new piece, first complete *Explore your piece*. You may want to fill in all the boxes in one go or spread your detective work over a week or two.

2 Warm up
Begin each practice session with some warm-ups. Your teacher will write some down on the warm-ups page for you to choose from.

3 Without music
Choose the piece you are going to focus on in your practice and deal yourself two to three cards from the 'Without music' pack. Work through the activities without looking at the music.

4 With music
Now (using the same piece) deal yourself between two to four cards from the 'With music' pack and work through those activities with the music open.

5 You choose
Complete your practice with a further activity of your own choice – playing one of your other pieces, some other scales, doing some sight-reading, composing a piece – and always be thinking about what the week's special feature might be (see page 20).

important

You may want to concentrate on just one piece in a practice session, or perhaps work at several. Deal yourself different cards for each piece.

Warm-ups

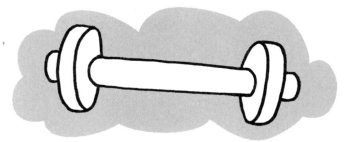

Ask your teacher to make a list of warm-ups for you to choose from when you begin each practice session (or see www.fabermusic.com/improve for some suggestions). These will include ideas on posture and hand position, playing without tension and a range of technical exercises.

Choose two or three warm-ups at the beginning of *every* practice session and spend at least two to three minutes on them.

Explore your piece

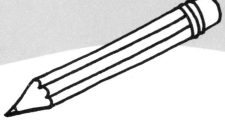

1 Title

2 Composer

3 Period

See page 24 for help

4 What does the title tell you about the music?

5 What key is the piece in?

6 Write the key signature here (including the clef)

7 Are there any scale and arpeggio patterns in the music?

8 In which bars do they occur?

9 What is the time signature?

10 What will you count?

All these answers form the 'ingredients' of your piece. If you don't understand a question, don't worry: just remember to ask your teacher in your next lesson.

11 Write down all the dynamics that occur, including *dim.* and *cresc.* List them in order of soft – loud:

12 Write down any other markings (such as staccato, slurs, accents etc.) and their meanings:

13 Write down some words that describe the mood of the piece:

14 Find out something interesting about the composer:

15 Are there any tricky rhythms in this piece?
Write them down here, and then clap them:

16 Is there anything particularly challenging in the piece?
Which bars will need special practice?

Explore your piece

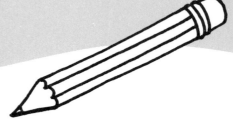

1 Title

2 Composer

3 Period

See page 24 for help

4 What does the title tell you about the music?

5 What key is the piece in?

6 Write the key signature here (including the clef)

7 Are there any scale and arpeggio patterns in the music?

8 In which bars do they occur?

9 What is the time signature?

10 What will you count?

6

11 Write down all the dynamics that occur, including *dim.* and *cresc.* List them in order of soft – loud:

12 Write down any other markings (such as staccato, slurs, accents etc.) and their meanings:

13 Write down some words that describe the mood of the piece:

14 Find out something interesting about the composer:

15 Are there any tricky rhythms in this piece?
Write them down here, and then clap them:

16 Is there anything particularly challenging in the piece?
Which bars will need special practice?

Explore your piece

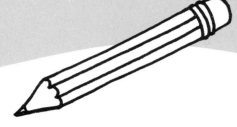

1 Title

2 Composer

3 Period

See page 24 for help

4 What does the title tell you about the music?

5 What key is the piece in?

6 Write the key signature here (including the clef)

7 Are there any scale and arpeggio patterns in the music?

8 In which bars do they occur?

9 What is the time signature?

10 What will you count?

11 Write down all the dynamics that occur, including *dim.* and *cresc.* List them in order of soft – loud:

12 Write down any other markings (such as staccato, slurs, accents etc.) and their meanings:

13 Write down some words that describe the mood of the piece:

14 Find out something interesting about the composer:

15 Are there any tricky rhythms in this piece? Write them down here, and then clap them:

16 Is there anything particularly challenging in the piece? Which bars will need special practice?

9

Explore your piece

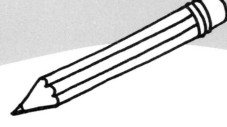

1 **Title**

2 **Composer**

3 **Period**

See page 24 for help

4 **What does the title tell you about the music?**

5 **What key is the piece in?**

6 **Write the key signature here (including the clef)**

7 **Are there any scale and arpeggio patterns in the music?**

8 **In which bars do they occur?**

9 **What is the time signature?**

10 **What will you count?**

11 Write down all the dynamics that occur, including
dim. and *cresc.* List them in order of soft – loud:

12 Write down any other markings (such as staccato, slurs,
accents etc.) and their meanings:

13 Write down some words that describe the mood of the piece:

14 Find out something interesting about the composer:

15 Are there any tricky rhythms in this piece?
Write them down here, and then clap them:

16 Is there anything particularly challenging in the piece?
Which bars will need special practice?

Explore your piece

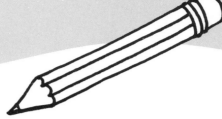

1 Title

2 Composer

3 Period

See page 24 for help

4 What does the title tell you about the music?

5 What key is the piece in?

6 Write the key signature here (including the clef)

7 Are there any scale and arpeggio patterns in the music?

8 In which bars do they occur?

9 What is the time signature?

10 What will you count?

What key is the piece in? Say the names of the notes of the scale up and down three times. Imagine yourself playing them.

Now play the scale slowly. Practise another scale you are learning in the same way.

Think about the title. What does it tell you about the character of the piece?

Now make up your own short piece with the same character, for either hand.

Clap or play any bar (or bars) that you can from memory.

Now make up a one-bar rhythm in the time signature of your piece, and clap it.

Find another piece (perhaps from your sight-reading book) that is in the same key or uses some of the same patterns as your piece. Study it silently, hearing it in your head as best you can. Practise any technical problems first. Feeling a strong, steady pulse, now play it through as accurately as possible.

Play the first two bars and the last two bars from memory. (Have a quick peek at the music if you can't remember them!)

Think about the character of the music you are about to play before you begin.

Choose a note (perhaps the first note of the piece) and play it *forte*. Listen to the sound very carefully as it dies away completely. Now sing the note. Now sing the note a tone above.

Make up a very short and simple tune (it could be based on a scale pattern).

Using section 11 of *Explore your piece*, play your tune at each of these dynamic levels.

What is the time signature of the piece?

Make up a simple rhythm (about four bars long) on one note, using this time signature. Write your rhythm down.

From *Explore your piece*, choose two or three ingredients and make up your own short and simple piece, lasting between 10 and 30 seconds. Think of a title first.

Practise the scale and arpeggio of the piece slowly with even rhythm and tone.

Now combine playing the scale and arpeggio with one ingredient from *Explore your piece*, for example a dynamic level, or a rhythm.

Using section 15 of *Explore your piece*, make up a short improvisation based on this rhythm. Use the right or left hand.

Using the keynote of the piece plus any other note, make gentle, angry, calm and humorous sounds (with one or both hands).

WITH MUSIC

Choose a bar from section 15 of *Explore your piece*. Make up some exercises to help you practise it, for example by repeating a pattern or changing the rhythm. Write the exercises down if you like.

WITH MUSIC

Choose four bars and play them:
- *ff*
- *pp*
- ◁ (*crescendo*)
- ▷ (*diminuendo*)
- as written
- from memory

WITH MUSIC

Reading the music, hear the piece through in your head as best you can. Can you find the phrases?

Can you make up a story to fit the music?

WITH MUSIC

Choose a tricky passage (one or two bars) and imagine yourself playing it. Now play it very slowly twenty times. Don't lose your concentration!

WITH MUSIC

Choose two or more bars and write them out, making some changes to the rhythm.

Play your new version. Use this as the start of an improvisation (which can be as short or as long as you like).

WITH MUSIC

Choose a short passage – look at it carefully, trying to hear it in your head. Now play it through slowly four times, the last time from memory.

WITH MUSIC

Play the piece (or part of the piece) through, *ignoring* all the dynamic markings.

Now play it again, *exaggerating* all the dynamic markings!

WITH MUSIC

Choose four bars (e.g. the final four) and practise them:
- very slowly
- with different rhythms
- with different dynamic markings
- at the correct tempo

Can you think of other ways to practise them?

WITH MUSIC

Choose a short passage (one or two bars) and play it an octave higher, then an octave lower than written. Use one or both hands.

Now sing the same passage at a comfortable pitch.

WITH MUSIC

With the right then the left hand, tap the rhythm of the whole piece on the closed lid of the piano. Include any dynamic markings.

WITH MUSIC

Choose as much, or as little, of the piece as you like. Prepare and then perform your chosen section. Decide if anything could be improved and perform it again.

WITH MUSIC

Tap the pulse with your foot and clap the rhythm of the right hand at the same time.

11 Write down all the dynamics that occur, including *dim.* and *cresc.* List them in order of soft – loud:

12 Write down any other markings (such as staccato, slurs, accents etc.) and their meanings:

13 Write down some words that describe the mood of the piece:

14 Find out something interesting about the composer:

15 Are there any tricky rhythms in this piece? Write them down here, and then clap them:

16 Is there anything particularly challenging in the piece? Which bars will need special practice?

Explore your piece

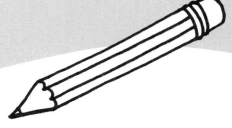

1 Title

2 Composer

3 Period

See page 24 for help

4 What does the title tell you about the music?

5 What key is the piece in?

6 Write the key signature here (including the clef)

7 Are there any scale and arpeggio patterns in the music?

8 In which bars do they occur?

9 What is the time signature?

10 What will you count?

11 Write down all the dynamics that occur, including
dim. and *cresc.* List them in order of soft – loud:

12 Write down any other markings (such as staccato, slurs,
accents etc.) and their meanings:

13 Write down some words that describe the mood of the piece:

14 Find out something interesting about the composer:

15 Are there any tricky rhythms in this piece?
Write them down here, and then clap them:

16 Is there anything particularly challenging in the piece?
Which bars will need special practice?

Explore your piece

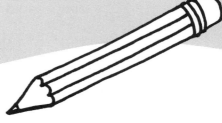

1. **Title**

2. **Composer**

3. **Period**

See page 24 for help

4. **What does the title tell you about the music?**

5. **What key is the piece in?**

6. **Write the key signature here (including the clef)**

7. **Are there any scale and arpeggio patterns in the music?**

8. **In which bars do they occur?**

9. **What is the time signature?**

10. **What will you count?**

11 Write down all the dynamics that occur, including *dim.* and *cresc.* List them in order of soft – loud:

12 Write down any other markings (such as staccato, slurs, accents etc.) and their meanings:

13 Write down some words that describe the mood of the piece:

14 Find out something interesting about the composer:

15 Are there any tricky rhythms in this piece? Write them down here, and then clap them:

16 Is there anything particularly challenging in the piece? Which bars will need special practice?

Explore your piece

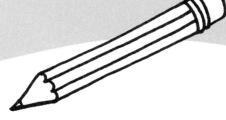

1 **Title**

2 **Composer**

3 **Period**

See page 24 for help

4 **What does the title tell you about the music?**

5 **What key is the piece in?**

6 **Write the key signature here (including the clef)**

7 **Are there any scale and arpeggio patterns in the music?**

8 **In which bars do they occur?**

9 **What is the time signature?**

10 **What will you count?**

11 Write down all the dynamics that occur, including *dim.* and *cresc.* List them in order of soft – loud:

12 Write down any other markings (such as staccato, slurs, accents etc.) and their meanings:

13 Write down some words that describe the mood of the piece:

14 Find out something interesting about the composer:

15 Are there any tricky rhythms in this piece?
Write them down here, and then clap them:

16 Is there anything particularly challenging in the piece?
Which bars will need special practice?

19

Practice diary

As your practice develops each week, decide on one special feature.
It may, for example, be one of the following:
- part or all of one of your pieces that you can play really well
- a technical challenge that you've overcome
- an improvisation (one that you can remember!)
- a particular scale you can play really well
- your own composition

Write it down in the table below and show it to your teacher.
It will become a very good starting point for the next lesson.

Week beginning	This week's special feature

Exam checklist

You may want to work through this section with your teacher.

Scales, arpeggios and broken chords
List all the scales etc. you need to know for the exam, or those that you are currently working on:

Aural
List the different tests you'll need to do:

Countdown to an exam

Tick each statement as soon as you feel it to be true! Award yourself a treat when all are ticked.

3 weeks to go ...

◯ I can play all my scales slowly but accurately, rhythmically and with a good and even tone.

◯ I'm practising sight-reading every day.

◯ I know exactly what the aural tests require me to do and have had a lot of help with them.

◯ I can play my pieces fairly fluently and with expression.

2 weeks to go ...

◯ I can play all my scales slowly but accurately and fluently.

◯ I'm practising sight-reading every day.

◯ I've had a lot of practice at the aural tests.

◯ I can play my pieces fluently, with expression and character.

1 week to go ...

◯ I can play all my scales accurately, fluently and confidently.

◯ I'm still practising sight-reading every day.

◯ I'm confident about the aural tests.

◯ I've performed all my pieces to friends/relatives confidently and with lots of musical expression and character.

1 day to go ...

◯ I'm really looking forward to the exam and am going to get a good night's sleep!

Useful stuff

Bear in mind that these dates are intended as a guide only.

Composer dates	Period
c.1425–1600	Renaissance
c.1600–1750	Baroque
c.1750–1820	CLASSICAL
c.1820–1915	Romantic
c.1915–2000	20th Century
2000 +	21st Century

Notes

Too tired to practise?

Then do one of the following activities instead:

1. Practise away from the piano – just sit down with the piece you're learning and hear it through in your head. Think particularly about the character.

2. Listen to some music – another piece by the same composer, a piece by another composer living at the same time, or some music in the same style. Your teacher will help.

3. Do a **PEP** analysis on the piece you are learning:
    P is for *problems* – decide what problems you still have to solve, technical or rhythmic for example. Make a note of them.
    E is for *expression* – what will you be trying to convey in your performance?
    P is for *practice* – the next practice! What in particular will you practise in your next session? Write your intentions down.